EVENTS
FOR THE YEAR
1983

To

....

Best wishes from

....

Your birth was one of the amazing events of 1983. Within these pages are some other interesting, earth-shattering moments of the year that was 1983.

Enjoy!

E V E N T S

THAT TOOK PLACE IN

JANUARY

- The British Nationality Act 1981 is put into effect, providing clarity as to the Citizenship of anyone born outside the UK to British parents.

- Danish fishermen challenge the British Government's ban on non-UK vessels angling in its waters.

- British armed police shoot and seriously injure Stephen Waldorf in a case of mistaken identity.

- The UK's first British breakfast time TV program, 'Breakfast Time', premiered on BBC1.

- The two police officers who injured Stephen Waldorf are accused of attempted murder and discharged on bail; they are suspended from duty pending further investigation.

- The ban on non-British fishing in British waters is lifted as the 'European Economic Community's Common Fisheries Policy' becomes effective.

- The 'Infrared Astronomical Satellite', the first space telescope able to survey the entire night sky is launched. The satellite is a joint undertaking between the

American space office NASA, the Netherlands Agency for Aerospace Programs and the UK's Science and Engineering Research Council.

Red rain falls in the UK, brought about by sand from the Sahara Desert.

Vehicle seat belts become mandatory for drivers and passengers.

- The New Jersey Transit Police Department is established in the state of New Jersey.

- The theatre production of Annie is performed for the last time on Broadway , New York City after 2,377 shows.

- Apple Inc. introduces the Apple Lisa personal computer.

- The spreadsheet program Lotus 1-2-3 is launched for IBM personal computers.

- The Washington Redskins rout the Miami Dolphins by a score of 27 – 17 in Super Bowl XVII at the Rose Bowl in Pasadena, California.

The Hawaiian volcano Kilauea starts erupting on the Big Island of Hawaii, and continues to flow for the next thirty years (On December 5, 2018, following 90 days of inertia the eruption that began in 1983 was pronounced to have finished).

The spreadsheet program Lotus 1-2-3 is launched for IBM personal computers.

E V E N T S

THAT TOOK PLACE IN

FEBRUARY

Work starts on broadening the Piccadilly line of London Underground at Heathrow Airport to serve the new Terminal 4.

- ITV franchise TV-am broadcasts for the first time.

- The UK joblessness figure peaks at a record high of 3,224,715.

- The dismembered remains of fifteen young men are found at a house in Muswell Hill, North London, casualties of seriel killer, Dennis Nilsen.

- The Austin Metro is the UK's best selling car.

- The Official Monster Raving Loony Party first challenges a local by-election.

- Patrick Jennings, 37 year-old Arsenal, and Northern Ireland goalkeeper becomes the first player in the English game to play in 1,000 senior football matches.

- Wah Mee slaughter: thirteen individuals are murdered in an attempted robbery in Seattle.

- The 'United States Environmental Protection Agency' takes action to clear the community of Times Beach, Missouri after it was found that toxic waste had been added to motor oil.

- Salem Nuclear Power Plant in New Jersey is decommissioned after a leak of radioactive water was discovered.

- Congress issues a report condemning the act of Japanese internment during World War II.

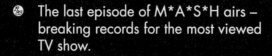

- The last episode of M*A*S*H airs – breaking records for the most viewed TV show.

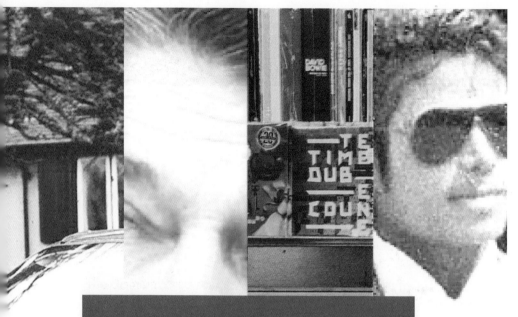

E V E N T S

THAT TOOK PLACE IN

M A R C H

The compact disc (CD) goes to market in the United Kingdom.

British Leyland starts selling the Austin Maestro, a five-door family hatchback car with a front-wheel-drive which replaces the canceled Maxi and Allegro.

In an attempt to stimulate the economy the government cuts taxes by £2 billion.

14

Liverpool wins the Football League Cup for the third year, beating Manchester United 2–1 in the final at Wembley Stadium.

Ian MacGregor is announced as leader of the National Coal Board.

American musician and songwriter Peter Ivers is bludgeoned to death in his home. The culprit is never discovered.

IBM drops the IBM PC XT.

'The Strategic Defense Initiative', otherwise known by the media as 'Star Wars' is announced. President Ronald Reagan proposes a defensive shield that would protect the United States from incoming enemy missiles.

Michael Jackson performs the ground breaking "Moonwalk" at a celebration of Motown's 25th anniversary.

Rob Lowe's film debut 'The Outsiders' is seen for the first time.

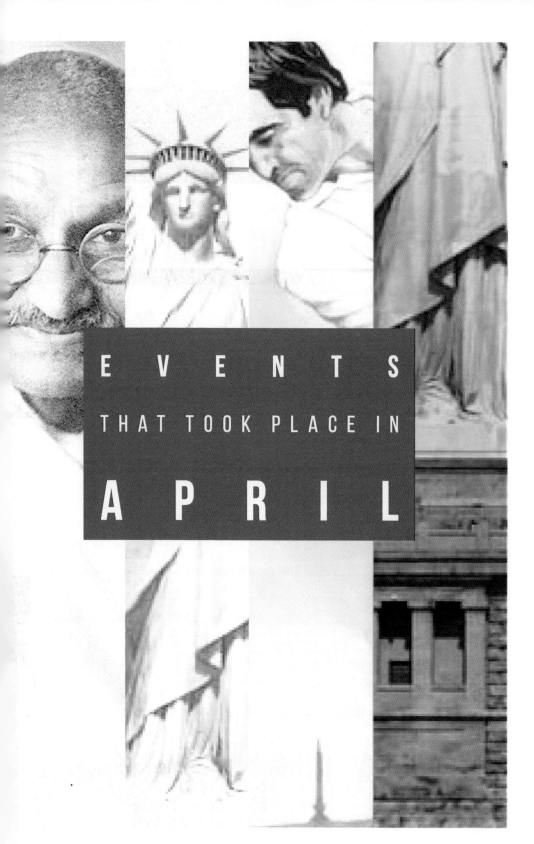

EVENTS THAT TOOK PLACE IN APRIL

Vauxhall releases the Nova supermini. It is the first Vauxhall to be manufactured outside the United Kingdom, being built at the Zaragoza plant in Spain where it was released seven months earlier in Europe as the Opel Corsa.

A 14-mile human chain protests in response to the siting of American atomic weapons in British army installations.

Three Russians are named as KGB agents by a Soviet renegade.

An armed robbery sees criminals escape with £7 million from a Security Express van in London.

Richard Attenborough's 1982 film Gandhi wins eight Academy Awards.

The one pound coin is launched in England and Wales.

- The April 1983 U.S. Embassy shelling in Beirut kills sixty three individuals.

- Maine student Samantha Smith is welcomed to the Soviet Union by General Secretary Yuri Andropov after he read her letter where she expressed her fears about nuclear war.

- New York Hockey right-winger Mike Bossy became first to score 60 goals in three consecutive seasons.

- David Copperfield makes the Statue of Liberty disappear in front of a live audience.

- Golfer Seve Ballesteros of Spain wins his second Masters championship.

- US President Reagan signs $165 billion Social Security pledge.

- In baseball, Nolan Ryan strikes out his 3,500th batter.

EVENTS

THAT TOOK PLACE IN

MAY

Margaret Thatcher calls a general election for 9 June.

Wheel clamps are used for the first time to battle prohibited parking in London.

Manchester United and Brighton & Hove Albion draw 2–2 in the FA Cup final at Wembley Stadium. The replay is held five days later.

Manchester United beat Brighton and Hove Albion 4–0 in the FA Cup replay at Wembley Stadium. Bryan Robson scores two of the goals.

Surveys suggest that the Conservatives are set to be re-elected with a landslide. A MORI survey puts them on 51% of the vote, 22% in front of Labour.

The Coalinga earthquake shook California causing many injuries and $10 million in losses.

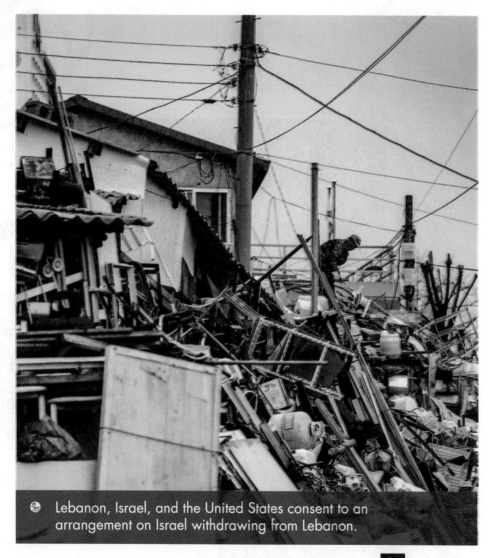

Lebanon, Israel, and the United States consent to an arrangement on Israel withdrawing from Lebanon.

● The 1983 NBA Finals, otherwise called Showdown '83, was the title round of the 1982–83 NBA season. The Philadelphia 76ers' crushed the Los Angeles Lakers 4 – 0. It was the last NBA Championship Series finished before June 1.

● National Missing Children's Day is announced by President Ronald Reagan, decisively four years after Etan Patz's vanishing.

● The ninth G7 summit starts at Williamsburg, Virginia.

24

EVENTS

THAT TOOK PLACE IN

JUNE

Jockey Lester Piggott triumphs at the Epsom Derby, his ninth win.

Margaret Thatcher, Conservative Prime Minister since 1979, wins a landslide victory over nearest rivals Labour. Among the new members of parliament are three Labour MP's, Tony Blair for Sedgefield in County Durham, Gordon Brown for Dunfermline East in Scotland and Jeremy Corbyn for Islington North in London.

Technology entrepreneur Clive Sinclair, creator of the Sinclair C5 is knighted.

Michael Foot leaves as the leader of the Labour Party. Neil Kinnock, the MP for Islwyn in South Wales is tipped to succeed him.

- Roy Jenkins leaves as the leader of the Social Democratic Party and is replaced by David Owen.

- The first episode of comedy Blackadder, starring Rowan Atkinson is broadcast on BBC One.

- The National Museum of Photography, Film, and Television opens in Bradford.

- Spacecraft Pioneer 10 is the first human made item to pass Planet Pluto and leave the Solar System.

- American Sally Ride is the first American woman to go into space, on the Space Shuttle Challenger.

- Betty White became the first woman to win a 'Daytime Emmy Award'.

- "Trading Places", starring Dan Ackroyd & Eddie Murphy is released.

- The Supreme Court changed the law on abortion.

In the US Open Men's Golf, Larry Nelson wins by one shot.

Space Shuttle Challenger safely flies back to Kennedy Space Center.

EVENTS
THAT TOOK PLACE IN
JULY

- New chancellor Nigel Lawson introduces public spending cuts of £500 million.

- Neil Kinnock escapes injury when his Ford Sierra crashes on the M4 motorway in Berkshire.

- Members of Parliament vote 361–245 against the reintroduction of capital punishment.

- Temperatures reach 33 °C in London.

- Twenty die when a British Airways Sikorsky S-61 helicopter crashes into the sea.

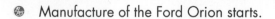

- A full size Tyrannosaurus Rex skeleton is erected for the first time at the Natural History Museum.

- Manufacture of the Ford Orion starts.

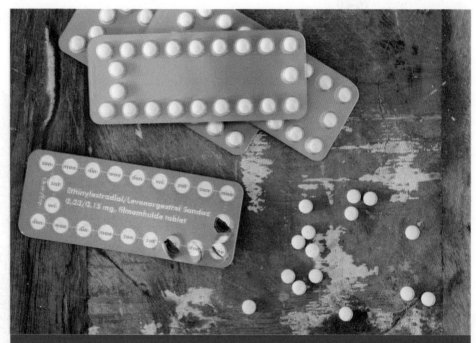

A Catholic mother of ten, Victoria Gillick loses a case in the High Court of Justice against the Government. She tried to stop the practice of contraceptives being given to youngsters younger than 16 without parental permission. The case later went to the House of Lords in 1985 when it was concluded that it is legal for doctors to recommend contraceptives to under-16s without parental assent in extraordinary conditions.

American schoolgirl, Samantha Smith flies into the Soviet Union as a guest of Yuri Andropov.

Wimbledon Women's Tennis: Martina Navratilova beats Andrea Jaeger 6-0, 6-3 for the fourth of nine Wimbledon singles titles.

- American Calvin Smith establishes new world record of 9.93 seconds for running 100 metres in Colorado Springs.

- Supreme Court rules equal retirement benefits for women.

- Storm stops Diana Ross' free show in New York's Central Park.

- Dick Smith makes first solo around the world helicopter ride.

Washington Public Power Supply System defaulted on $2.25 billion of municipal bonds making it the biggest default in history.

NASA sent Telstar-3A Communications Satellite into space.

"Friday Night Videos" debuts on NBC TV.

EVENTS

THAT TOOK PLACE IN

AUGUST

The new A-prefix vehicle licence plates are released, helping stimulate vehicle sales following the drop in sales brought about by the recession.

Twenty two Provisional Irish Republican Army (IRA) members receive jail sentences totaling more than 4,000 years from a Belfast Court.

Temperatures hit 30 °C in London.

ITV releases the popular TV show, 'Blockbusters', a game show hosted by Bob Holness.

America West Airlines starts services out of Phoenix, Arizona, and Las Vegas, Nevada.

Storm Alicia hits the Texas coast, killing 22 and causing over US$3.8 billion in damage.

The Old Philadelphia Sporting Arena is destroyed by fire.

Space Shuttle Challenger ferries Guion Bluford, the first African-American space traveler, into space.

BIRM
UNIV
MED
(Lect

CONF
£3 i:

APPL
M
S:
M
B:

CONF

Medic
W
2 To:

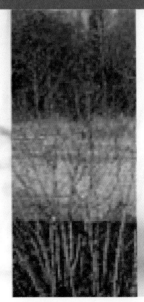

E V E N T S

THAT TOOK PLACE IN

SEPTEMBER

● Ian MacGregor becomes chairman of the National Coal Board.

NUCLEAR WAR AND THE N.H.S.

A
Conference for
Nurses and Other
Health Workers

BIRMINGHAM
UNIVERSITY
MEDICAL SCHOOL
(Lecture Room 6)

SATURDAY
15TH OCTOBER 1983
9.30 - 4.30

CONFERENCE FEE:-
£5   includes tea & coffee but not lunch

APPLY TO:-
Mary Ann Reynolds,
65 Cotton Lane,
Moseley,
Birmingham B13 9SE.

CONFERENCE ORGANISED BY:-
Medical Campaign Against Nuclear
Weapons,
7 Tenison Road,
Cambridge CB1 2DG.

● The National Health Service (NHS) privatises cleaning, catering, and laundry services in a move which Social Services Secretary Norman Fowler predicts will save between £90 million and £180 million per year.

● The Social Democratic Party Conference casts a ballot against a merger with the Liberals until at least 1988.

● The England national football team lose 1–0 to Denmark at Wembley Stadium in the penultimate qualifying game for Euro 84, making qualification impossible.

● Docklands redevelopment in East London starts with the opening of an Enterprise Zone on the Isle of Dogs.

🌑 Maze Prison escape: Thirty eight IRA detainees armed with six guns seize a lorry and break out of HM Prison Maze in County Antrim, Northern Ireland, the biggest prison escape since World War II and in British history. Nineteen escapees are later arrested.

🌑 In the most recent crackdown on football hooliganism, seven men are imprisoned for aggressive behaviour at a game.

● Cold War: Korean Air Lines Flight 007 is shot down by a Soviet Union jet fighter when the commercial airplane enters Soviet airspace. Every one of the 269 passengers on board dies including U.S. Congressman Larry McDonald.

● Tom Brokaw turns into the lead anchor for NBC Nightly News.

● Vanessa Lynn Williams is the first African-American to be crowned Miss America, in Atlantic City, New Jersey.

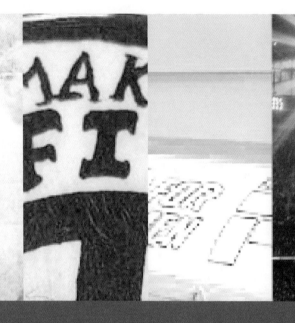

EVENTS
THAT TOOK PLACE IN
OCTOBER

- Ford launches two pivotal new models - a facelifted rendition of the Fiesta supermini, and the Orion, which is a saloon variant of the Escort.

- Neil Kinnock is chosen to head the Labour Party following the retirement of Michael Foot. Kinnock pulled in over 70% of the votes, and names Roy Hattersley as his deputy.

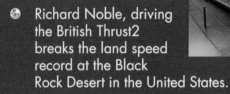

- Richard Noble, driving the British Thrust2 breaks the land speed record at the Black Rock Desert in the United States.

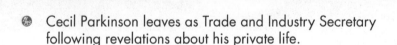

- Cecil Parkinson leaves as Trade and Industry Secretary following revelations about his private life.

- The shooting of Stephen Waldorf: The two Metropolitan police officers who shot and injured Stephen Waldorf in January are cleared of attempted murder.

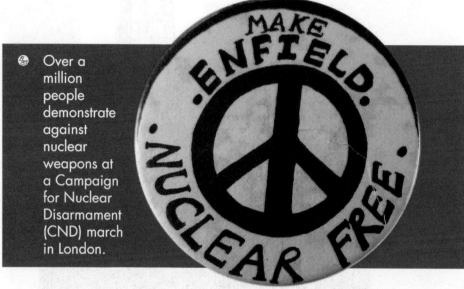

- Over a million people demonstrate against nuclear weapons at a Campaign for Nuclear Disarmament (CND) march in London.

- Dennis Nilsen goes on trial at the Central Criminal Court blamed for six murders and two attempted murders. He admits to killing up to "15 or 16" men.

World Series: The Baltimore Orioles rout the Philadelphia Phillies 5–0 in Game five, to win the SERIES 4 games to 1 for their third World Championship.

Concurrent suicide truck-bombings hit both the French and the United States Marine Corps dormitory in Beirut, killing 241 U.S. members of the armed forces, 58 French paratroopers, and six Lebanese citizens.

US troops attack Grenada.

Microsoft Word is first launched.

An earthquake measuring 6.9 shook central Idaho.

E V E N T S

THAT TOOK PLACE IN

NOVEMBER

Dennis Nilsen is sentenced to life in prison.

Five divers on the Byford Dolphin semi-submersible drilling rig are killed while boring in the Frigg gas field in the North Sea.

The first United States cruise rockets arrive at RAF Greenham Common in Berkshire amid protests from peace campaigners.

48

- Gerry Adams is appointed as head of Sinn Fein.

- England beat Luxembourg 4–0 in their last Euro 84 qualifying game yet at the same time fail to qualify for the following summer's competition in France. Hooliganism mars the end of the match.

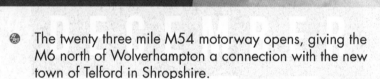

- Thirty-one year-old Liverpool lady Janet Walton gives birth to sextuplets following fertility treatment.

- The twenty three mile M54 motorway opens, giving the M6 north of Wolverhampton a connection with the new town of Telford in Shropshire.

- The Brink's-Mat robbery occurred In London when 6,800 gold bars worth about £26 million are taken from the Brink's-Mat vault at Heathrow Airport. Just a small amount of the gold is ever recovered, and only two men are sentenced for the robbery.

Martin Luther King Day: At the White House Rose Garden, U.S. President Ronald Reagan signs a bill establishing a government holiday on the third Monday of each January in respect of American social equality pioneer Martin Luther King Jr. It was first observed in 1986.

The Reverend Jesse Jackson declares his intention to stand for the 1984 Democratic Party presidential election.

Ronald Reagan is the first U.S. President to address the Japanese government.

The immunosuppressant Cyclosporine is endorsed by the FDA, prompting innovation in the field of transplantation.

The anti-cancer medication Etoposide is approved for use in the battle against testicular carcinoma.

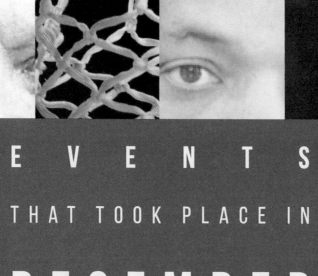

E V E N T S

THAT TOOK PLACE IN

DECEMBER

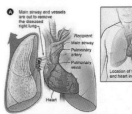

- An SAS covert operation comes to an end in the shooting of two IRA terrorists.

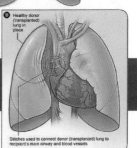

- First heart and lung transplant performed in Britain at Harefield.

- The House of Lords votes to permit the broadcast of its day to day activities.

- An IRA car bomb murders six, three police and three civilians, and injures ninety outside Harrods in London.

- A subsequent IRA bomb detonates in Oxford Street, but this time no one is harmed.

- William Golding wins the Nobel Prize in Literature.

53

EVENTS
FOR THE YEAR
1983

- Michael Jackson's music video for "Thriller" is aired for the first time.

- Lt. Bobby Goodman of the United States Navy is shot down over Lebanon and caught by the Syrians.

- Apple Macintosh advertisement is launched.

- The Detroit Pistons defeated the Denver Nuggets for an NBA record 370, with Detroit winning in triple extra time, 186–184.

- A propane blast in Buffalo, New York kills five firefighters and two civilians.

🌀 The Reverend Jesse Jackson goes to Syria to secure the release of U.S. Naval force Lieutenant Robert Goodman, who has been in Syrian imprisonment since being shot down during an observation mission.

TOP 10 SINGLES FOR 1983

UK

TOP 10 SINGLES FOR 1983

1 **Karma Chameleon**
by Culture Club

2 **Uptown Girl**
by Billy Joel

3 **Red Red Wine**
by UB40

4 **Wherever I Lay My Hat (That's My Home)**
by Paul Young

5 **True**
by Spandau Ballet

6 **Every Breath You Take**
by The Police

7 **Baby Jane**
by Rod Stewart

8 **Down Under**
by Men At Work

9 **Give It Up**
by KC & The Sunshine Band

10 **Let's Dance**
by David Bowie

US

TOP 10 SINGLES FOR 1983

1 **Maneater**
by Daryl Hall & John Oates

2 **The girl is mine**
by Michael Jackson / Paul McCartney

3 **Dirty laundry**
by Don Henley

4 **Down Under**
by Men At Work

5 **Sexual Healing**
by Marvin Gaye

6 **Mickey**
by Toni Basil

7 **Gloria**
by Laura Branigan

8 **Steppin out**
by Joe Jackson

9 **Rock this town**
by The Stray Cats

10 **Truly**
by Lionel Richie

TOP ALBUMS FOR 1983

UK

TOP ALBUMS FOR 1983

1 **Synchronicity**
by The Police

2 **Can't Slow Down**
by Lionel Richie

3 **Flashdance**
by Original Soundtrack

4 **Color by Numbers**
by Culture Club

5 **Let's Dance'**
David Bowie

6 **The Final Cut**
by Pink Floyd

7 **An Innocent Man**
by Billy Joel

8 **Genesis**
by Genesis

9 **War**
by U2

10 **Eliminator**
by ZZ Top

US
TOP ALBUMS FOR 1983

1 **Synchronicity**
by The Police

2 **Thriller**
by Michael Jackson

3 **Flashdance**
by Original Soundtrack

4 **Pyromania**
by Def Leppard

5 **The Wild Heart**
by Stevie Nicks

6 **Staying Alive**
by Bee Gees

7 **An Innocent Man**
by Billy Joel

8 **Alpha**
by Asia

9 **Lawyers in Love**
by Jackson Browne

10 **Reach the Beach**
by The Fixx

TOP GROSSING MOVIES FOR 1983

UK
TOP GROSSING MOVIES FOR 1983

1. Octopussy
2. Never Say Never Again
3. Superman III
4. Yentl
5. Krull
6. Monty Python's The Meaning of Life
7. Educating Rita
8. Local Hero
9. The Dresser
10. The Hunger

US

TOP GROSSING MOVIES FOR 1983

1 Star Wars Ep. VI: Return of the Jedi

2 Terms of Endearment

3 Flashdance

4 Trading Places

5 WarGames

6 Octopussy

7 Sudden Impact

8 Mr. Mom

9 Staying Alive

10 Risky Business

SPORTING HIGHLIGHTS FOR 1983

Yannick Noah won the French Open for the only grand slam title of his career. Though he has 23 titles to his name, it never translated into more grand slam success.

Martina Navratilova had another spectacular season with three grand slam titles, missing out only on the French Open.

Tom Watson won the British Open for his eighth and final major. His total wins have since been surpassed only by two golfers thus far.

Patty Sheehan won the LPGA Championship for the first of her six majors.

Jimmy Connors won his eighth and final grand slam title in the US Open defeating the then-upcoming player **Ivan Lendl**.

Arthur Ashe underwent bypass surgery in June of that year during which he contracted HIV, which eventually lead to his death in 1993.

Laurent Fignon of France won the Tour de France for the first time. Fignon would also successfully defend his title the following year.

Greg LeMond was an upcoming rider at the time, and he won the Road Championship that year to become the only American to achieve the feat. LeMond would go on to have great success in the Tour de France later in his career.

COST OF LIVING IN 1983

COST OF LIVING IN THE UK IN 1983

- Average House Price **£34,795**

- A gallon of Petrol **£1.25**

- Yearly Inflation Rate UK **4.6%**

- Interest Rates Year End Bank of England **9.06%**

COST OF LIVING IN THE USA IN 1983

- Yearly Inflation Rate USA **3.22%**

- Year-End Close Dow Jones Industrial Average **1258**

- Interest Rates Year End Federal Reserve **11.00%**

- Average Cost of new house **$82,600**

- Average Income per year **$21,070.00**

- Average Monthly Rent **$335.00**

POPULAR NAMES OF 1983

TOP 10
MALE NAMES

1. Michael
2. Christopher
3. Matthew
4. David
5. Joshua
6. James
7. Jason
8. Daniel
9. John
10. Robert

TOP 10
FEMALE NAMES

1. Jennifer
2. Jessica
3. Amanda
4. Ashley
5. Sarah
6. Melissa
7. Nicole
8. Stephanie
9. Heather
10. Elizabeth

- IBM releases the IBM PC XT

- Strategic Defense Initiative (SDI) Proposed

- Harrods Bombing

- Space Shuttle Challenger has its maiden flight

- Microsoft Word is launched

- Following on from the start of the recession in the US, Unemployment Rises to 12 million

- The US starts deploying Cruise Missiles and Pershing Missiles to Europe at the Greenham Common Air Force Base in England and West Germany amid mass protest

- Sally Ride became the first woman in space

- The UK introduced its first one pound coin

- The US Congress initiated its War Powers Act for the first time.

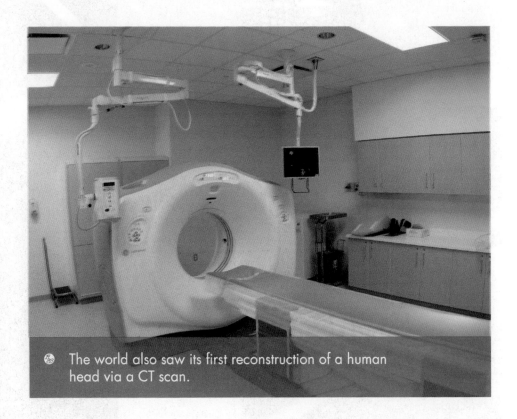

The world also saw its first reconstruction of a human head via a CT scan.

PRESIDENT RONALD REAGAN
PROPOSES THE STRATEGIC DEFENSE INITIATIVE (SDI).

1. U.S. President Ronald Reagan publicly proposes the Strategic Defense Initiative (SDI) during a televised address in March of 1983.

2. The proposed defense system was a highly advanced system that would rely on technology that had not yet been developed to intercept and prevent a nuclear missile attack on the U.S. by the Soviet Union.

3. The plan was called "Star Wars" by many critics who thought it impossible to introduce due to the limited technology available at the time.

4. SDI began development in the following year under the Department of Defense but its funding ended after the Cold War ended and before anything could be completed.

THE LIFE AND DEATH OF
KAREN CARPENTER
WHO DIED IN FEBRUARY 1983

EVENTS
FOR THE YEAR
1983

Karen Carpenter along with her older brother, Richard formed the singing duo known as The Carpenters. She is considered by many to have had one of the greatest singing voices of all time. She sadly passed away in 1983 at the age of 32 from a condition linked to her Anorexia.

Siblings Richard and Karen Carpenter were born to make music together, and their beautiful harmonies, and Karen's stunning vocals have made them a legendary act.

SOME OF THEIR VERY BEST SONGS WERE:

1. (They Long to be) Close to you.
2. We've Only Just Begun
3. Superstar
4. Rainy days and Mondays
5. Yesterday Once More
6. Ticket to Ride
7. For All We Know
8. Goodbye to Love
9. Top of the World
10. Calling Occupants of Interplanetary Craft

To ....

Best wishes from

....

Your birth was one of the
amazing events of 1983.
Within these pages are
some other interesting,
earth-shattering moments
of the year that was 1983.

Enjoy!

Printed in Great Britain
by Amazon

24673071R00043